A Hike

by William Overturf
illustrated by Jane McCreary

Practice Decodable 83

Mc Graw Hill Education

Bothell, WA • Chicago, IL • Columbus, OH • New York, NY

MHEonline.com

Send all inquiries to:
McGraw-Hill Education
8787 Orion Place
Columbus, OH 43240

ISBN: 978-0-02-145738-0
MHID: 0-02-145738-7

Printed in China.

8 9 10 11 12 DSS 27 26 25 24 23

The rain stopped. The hikers looked at the trail. Would it be muddy? Did the rain spoil it?

"The trail looks fine," said Lily. She was the leader.

Lily looked at her wrist. "And we have time."

Lily smiled at the hikers.

"Now we can try to hike, boys and girls," she said in a happy voice.

Lily used her cell phone to call camp.
"My idea is to keep hiking," she said.

The sun was shining now. And there was a rainbow! Kids took photos of it. They enjoyed the hike.

The kids saw a lighthouse. By the lighthouse, waves hit big, big rocks. The waves made a loud noise.

At night, the lighthouse helped ships. It helped ships avoid the big rocks.

"Those rocks could wreck a ship!" cried Phil.

"They have," said Lily.

Lily said more. "A ship filled with gold coins hit the rocks. It was destroyed. The sailors were safe."

"A sailor wrote about the wreck," said Lily.
"Lots of gold coins were sunk by the rocks."

Lily pointed as the five hikers looked at the beach. "Waves still bring gold coins to the beach."

Phil looked at the sandy soil. He saw a shiny, bright thing. Was it a gold coin?

Phil ran to the shiny thing. It did look like gold! Phil tried to take a close look at the tiny item.

It was just an old candy wrapper. It was made of gold foil.

Lily smiled. So did Phil.